$2,000 An Hour

Claim A Share of Your $25,000,000,000 The U.S. Gov't Holds

David Bendah

This publication is designed to provide accurate and authorative information in regard to the subject matter covered. It is sold with the understanding that the publisher is not engaged in rendering legal, accounting, or other professional service. If legal advice or other expert assistance is required the services of a competent professional should be sought.

Some of the methods presented in this book may be illegal in certain parts of the United States. This book is sold for informational purposes only.

Typesetting by Typecast Graphics of San Diego

ISBN 0-933301-10-3

Contributions

I would like to make special mention of the talented people who made this book a success.

Gary Silver—Main research contributor as well as assisting in the discovery of the process.

Tracey Weddleton—Copy editor and proofreader.

Michele Howard—Assisted with various organizational functions.

Dedications

To my brother:

Morris Bendah

To my close friends:

Sam Glassman

Lloyd San

Brad Cohen

Table Of Contents

Chapter 1

Your $25 Billion Opportunity

I'm becoming wealthier every hour and I am feeling great about it. You can do the same with my amazing new discovery. I will show you a unique method of making money with little or no effort. It is an opportunity that has never been disclosed before. All you need is a telephone, a directory, and the very book you hold, and you're ready to make big money.

You may be thinking that I have always been wealthy but I must tell you — life was not always rosy. About two years ago, I was involved in a bad business investment. I had lost over $11,000 in a matter of weeks. Everything I owned or had was taken away from me. I was desperate. I worked as a clerk by day and a waiter at night — I never really liked cleaning tables, but what else could I do? I felt I was a disappointment to my loved ones. I remember coming home on Mother's Day anxious to call my mother — only to find my phone had been disconnected. I went through my mail and prayed for some good news — only to find a strange-looking envelope with no return address — it was my eviction notice. Fortunately, my relatives were kind enough to let me stay with them. I had no idea being in debt could hurt so much; I prayed for a way out.

In my depth of despair, I received a strange letter. I thought it was just another creditor making a claim on me. But this letter informed me of money that I could receive. It said if I signed the enclosed form, I would receive $2,592.59. At this point I had nothing to lose, so I neatly signed the form and sent it back to the company. Ten days later, a check for $2,592.59 came in the mail with an explanation. A distant aunt had died and left $4,320.98 in her savings account. The agency that located me collected $1,728.39. It wasn't even difficult for the agency to find that I was related to her. I was so excited; I wanted to find out more about this great opportunity. This agency was making millions of dollars by simply matching up people with their names in the phone book.

One-third of all Americans have forgotten or lost their money in bank accounts, stocks, insurance premiums, etc. An incredible $25 billion dollars has been 'lost' — that's as much as the amount of $10 bills you could stack around the world. If your income were $10 million a year, you still wouldn't be able to dent this huge amount of money.

$25 Billion

Twenty-five billion dollars are just sitting there waiting for you to recover it. I picked up three phone directories and began making simple phone calls. I contacted an 81-year-old Virginia widow. Her husband had left $61,251 in a bank account 20 years earlier. She had an unlisted phone number, but her address was in an earlier phone book. She lived at the same address for 50 years. A certified letter informed her of her money. The finder's fee for that job was $20,416 — not bad for 30 minutes of work. Imagine my shock of getting paid so much just to look up a name in the phone book. And you don't have to be smart to do what I did — I made it through high school with a C-minus average. By no means was I ever considered to be a genius. Yet, all I did was thumb through the phone book and make a few phone calls — it was that easy. And the efforts have paid off, too.

My family and I have always loved the coast, so during the summer we moved into a $250,000 home by the beach. The money I was earning from tracking down rightful owners of their unclaimed cash was adding up — rapidly. Last month I deposited over $30,000. Just as a hedge against taxes, I bought two three-bedroom houses valued at $200,000. I asked my family what they wanted most; they wanted to explore places together. In the past month we have visited three countries, and we can take a vacation every month if we desire. It's great seeing the joy in my family's eyes when we spend time together — all of this because I looked up a few names and made a few calls. And there are plenty of opportunities for you to find the owners of lost property or money.

Only 10 percent of the rightful owners claim their $25 billion. The states, not surprisingly, make no real effort to contact the rightful owners. Why should they when unclaimed property is their biggest source of revenue, second only to taxes?

Unclaimed money has been around a long time. As long as man could lose money he would create an unclaimed account. Just to emphasize this point I have clipped out an article from a 1922 San Francisco Chronicle newspaper. The article talks about how much unclaimed money is left in San Francisco banks.

Locating Your People

How hard is it to locate an individual who owns unclaimed property? A California bank had an unclaimed property list with Bob Hope and Lucille Ball on it. You see, banks, insurance companies and other institutions would rather make interest on your money than find you and return it. But they are still required by law to publish these names. Very few people read these lists, and this is what makes this

C SAN FRANCISCO CHRONICLE,

$750,000 Deposits Go Unclaimed in S.F. Banks

Neglected Riches for State After 20 Years

Figures Hide Stories of Human Tragedies

San Francisco banks rapidly are completing their respective reports of deposits unclaimed during the ten and twenty years preceding January 1, 1921. Banking authorities here say that the sum will approximate $750,000. This estimate largely is based on the fact that deposits unclaimed during the ten and twenty years preceding January 1, 1919, totaled $420,957.48.

The law provides that every bank in California shall make an annual report of deposits unclaimed during the twenty years preceding the date of said report. It also provides that, in odd years, the banks shall make additional reports, showing the deposits unclaimed during the preceding ten years.

PROVISION OF LAW

In this connection the law stipulates that:

"All amounts of money heretofore, or hereafter deposited with any bank to the credit of depositors who have not made a deposit on said account, or withdrawn any part thereof, or the interest, and which shall have remained unclaimed for more than twenty years after the date of such deposit, or withdrawal of any part of principal or interest, and where neither the depositor nor any claimant has filed any notice with such bank showing his or her present residence, shall, with the increase and proceeds thereof, escheat to the State."

Pursuant to this provision, the Attorney-General of the State is charged with the duty of taking the proper steps to insure the turning over of this money to the State treasury. This means that through carelessness, neglect, death or some other exigency, something like $75,000, deposited more than twenty years ago in the banks of San Francisco, shortly will be paid over by these banks to the State. Each year the amount increases, indicating, if one cares to analyze the matter, increasing thoughtlessness on the part of the people.

PENCHANT FOR WASTING

In these latter days, when thinking men and women throughout the country earnestly are seeking to impress upon the minds of every one—but especially the youth of the land—the value of thrift, the eloquent story told by San Francisco banks is one that should challenge undivided interest. Certainly there is much in the story told by these reports of deposits unclaimed to support the contention that the American people, young and old, display a remarkable penchant for wasting.

Carelessness in handling what one has is on a par with the distinctly American characteristic of acting on the principle that want never can overtake one. If this brand of carelessness ever has been exemplified in San Francisco, it would seem to have been in the apparently utter disregard for literally thousands of accounts, small and large, forgotten in the banks of this city.

HUMAN INTEREST

What a hidden wealth of human interest essentially lies in the emotionless columns of figures comprising the San Francisco bank reports of deposits unclaimed during the last twenty years. Here, if anywhere, comedy must have stalked hand in hand with tragedy. It requires no effort of the imagination to speculate on the close relationship that must have existed between those forgotten deposits and the everyday life of the community as depicted in the newspaper accounts of those days.

Perusal of the reports submitted by the various banks brings to light much of interest. The forgotten accounts range in amounts anywhere from one cent to thousands of dollars. Obviously, before these reports are submitted every effort is made by the banks to locate the depositors. In some cases they are found to have died, leaving no trace of possible heirs, while in still other instances they simply have disappeared.

HEAVY TASK FOR BANKS

The work necessarily devolving upon the banks in caring for these forgotten accounts is tremendous. In times gone by, this work oftentimes was compensated for by the banks having been permitted to retain unclaimed deposits. While any of these banks gladly would have paid deposits to persons able to establish bona fide ownership, the sums that thus came into possession of various banks throughout the country were considerable. It is related that in Cleveland, more than one palatial bank building was erected solely through use of unclaimed deposits.

Not all deposits unclaimed during a period of ten years necessarily remain unclaimed during the ensuing ten years. Bank officials here declare that many deposits are claimed between the ten and twenty-year period. Most such deposits have been forgotten, but occasionally, so bank officials say, men and women purposely have permitted their accounts to remain untouched for long periods of time.

VARIED ACCOUNTS

Analysis of the various reports shows that not all of the unclaimed deposits are personal accounts. Fraternal and political organizations are numbered among the depositors. Numerous accounts are shown in the name of trustees. Families widely-known in California are numbered among those depositors in San Francisco banks who apparently have forgotten the existence of their respective accounts.

In the Fresno branch of the Bank of Italy, for instance, are accounts credited to Mrs. F. Cartwright, George Barclay Hodgkin and George Shirley. In the Los Angeles branch the Non-Partisan City Central Committee, Myer Lissner, secretary, is credited with an account of $37.72. Los Angeles Tent No. 2, Knights of the Maccabees, is credited with a deposit of $796.38. Florence E. Dolph has an account of $1701.93 and Blanche L. Dolph has a credit of $2763.51.

The Wells Fargo Nevada National Bank of San Francisco shows an account of $13.50 credited to the American Bank of Mexico, while the Bar Association of San Francisco has an account of $3.80. The National Biscuit Co. still has a deposit of $1.88 that has not been touched during the last ten years.

BALANCE OF ONE CENT

In the Merchants' National Bank, Gus Bouquest still has an undisturbed balance of one cent that may go to the State unless prompt action be taken. The Swedish Christian Benevolent Society has a deposit of $23.59 that faces the same fate. John J. Ortner, trustee for Fred H. Ortner, has an account of $11.68 in the San Francisco Savings and Loan Society and Alexander McKenzie has $2223.64 in the same institution. In the Union Trust Company of San Francisco, A. L. Anderson has an undisturbed deposit of $2702.63 while Lillie B. Crocker, executrix of the estate of Mina D. Solomon, has $219.48 in this institution.

In the reports thus far received by the State Superintendent of Banks, the smallest unclaimed deposit is one cent, while the largest, $7883.66. For the most part the individual items shown in the various reports are for small amounts, the average being deposits of approximately $1.50.

A 1922 San Francisco Chronical newspaper article that talks about unclaimed money in San Francisco Banks.

business so easy. I will show you how to get these lists which, in many cases, are free.

Look at what someone who has never done a search was able to do. Bonnie Goldstien, a writer for the San Francisco Chronicle who doesn't know that much about finding people, located the owners of $4,100 in two-and-a-half hours with two telephone directories. All you need is a phone book, library references and some time to make yourself a fortune. I'll show you exactly how to find people on unclaimed property lists.

To make your quest for unclaimed money easier, I have information about advanced systems of searching for people that only the top private investigators and government security organizations use. You will be amazed at how easy it is to find anyone you want — no matter where this person is.

How Much Could You Make?

In California, the owner of one account — worth $186,000 — still hasn't been found. Someone in Massachusetts left behind $400,000. A North Carolina resident still hasn't claimed his or her $500,000. You can retire by finding only one unclaimed property owner — just one — and you are set for life. I was able to buy a new bi-level three-bedroom house with the money I received by just finding one owner. You can do the same. There is a treasure of $25 billion waiting for you. And this treasure increases by one billion dollars every year. Do you know that if this money were to be disbursed to everyone living in Canada, every Canadian would get more than $1,000? If you were to make $10,000,000 a year, you wouldn't even be able to dent this huge pot of gold. And this gold is waiting for you. The best thing about it is that I am going to show you how to get it. Follow the instructions in this book, and you could have riches beyond your wildest desires.

Chapter 2

Getting The Bills Rolling

It sounds hard to believe that people leave thousands of dollars in banks and other institutions and then forget about it. I know I would have a hard time doing that. But the truth is that it happens all the time. Your goal is to contact the owners of this unclaimed money and collect a fee for your services. There are people doing just that and are making a hefty profit every year.

Every state has an unclaimed property office that has the sole responsibility of returning unclaimed money back to its owners. Every state has different laws and policies regarding the handling of unclaimed money. Let me first explain the process of how money is left unclaimed. A person, due to neglect, forgetfulness or death will leave behind money in an institution. The institution, whether it be a bank, insurance company, business (retirement fund), government office, or even a security company, must report unclaimed money to the state. If the unclaimed money is not claimed by the owner in a specified period of time (the amount of time varies from state to state; in California it is five to seven years, depending on the institution), this money must be turned over to the state treasury department. Some states

EXHIBIT I

THE UNCLAIMED PROPERTY PROGRAM

The Unclaimed Property Law is designed to return unclaimed property to owners or to their heirs. These people have either forgotten about the property, or in some instances did not even know of its existence.

The State does not receive any of this "abandoned" property until it has been held by the organizations reporting it for seven years after the last contact with the named owners.

The State begins its efforts to contact the owners as soon as the property is reported to us. The State Controller publishes the names of owners in a newspaper in the county of their last known address. In addition, the State Controller also mails a notice to the named owners at their last known address.

Current lists are also distributed to main libraries and interested TV and radio stations.

Microfilmed records of all accounts that have not been claimed are maintained in our office and are open for public review on Wednesdays and Thursdays from 8:00 to 4:30 p.m. These microfilmed records have also been made available for purchase. (See Exhibit "3" for cost and ordering instructions.)

The success of the unclaimed property program is evident. Last year alone, almost $10 million dollars were restored to owners as a result of program effort.

* * * *

In addition to unclaimed property, we also receive Estates of Deceased Persons. These come to us under provision of the Probate Code. Microfilmed listings of the estates are also available for review or purchase. (See Exhibit "3" for cost). Unlike abandoned property accounts, which are held in perpetuity, these estates do permanently escheat after a period of time and are no longer available to claim after a specified date.

Estates with named heirs in the amount of $1,000 or greater are subject to judicial escheat. After we have held the money received on these estates for a period of five years, we send a list to the Attorney General's Office. Their office publishes the list, again verifies with us that there has been no activity on the account, then initiates a court order to affect permanent escheat. Five years from the date of this order we then complete the escheat action. Thus, on these estates the property is subject to claim for 10 years after receipt of funds by our office.

Estates with named heirs under $1,000 and all estates with no named heirs are subject to administrative escheat. The estates under $1,000 with known heirs escheat 10 years after we receive the money - the estates with no known heirs escheat 5 years after receipt of money.

We publish a legal notice listing the estates under $1,000 with known heirs in the San Francisco, Sacramento and Los Angeles areas.

The above escheated actions are reversible if it can be demonstrated that an inquiry or claim was initiated before the escheat date.

* * *

The State of California's unclaimed property policy.

have no time restriction for a person to claim his or her money once it is in the hands of the state, but some states do have time restrictions. Wyoming only allows owners five years to claim their money, while states like Indiana allow owners 25 years.

One more thing to remember is that some states pay interest on unclaimed money (not more than 5 percent). However, most states don't pay interest on the unclaimed money that's sitting in their accounts.

Contacting the State Offices

The state offices contain a gold mine of information. They have lists of owners of unclaimed property that they will give to you just for the asking. Lists are also available at many public libraries. You may want to call your library to see if you can have access to their lists.

In addition to unclaimed property, the states also receive estates of deceased persons. Listings of the estates are also available for review or purchase. Unlike abandoned property accounts — which are held in perpetuity — these estates do permanently escheat after a period of time and are no longer available to claim after a specified date. In legal jargon, if an estate is subject to 'escheat,' it means that the state has the authority to take the money permanently if the rightful heirs don't claim it within a set number of years.

Contact your state office or any state office of unclaimed property and see what you have to do to get a list of unclaimed property owners from them. The unclaimed property office in your state must let you have access to this list. According to the Freedom of Information Act of 1966, you have the right to view any public document, and an unclaimed property list is a public document. Be persistent. Once you have viewed this list, the rest is simple.

Some state offices may not send you the list of names, or they may charge you a large fee. There's a way around this, though. Go to your state's unclaimed property office in per-

CLASS CODE

CODE TYPE OF ORGANIZATION	CODE TYPE OF INTANGIBLE PROPERTY
Banking Organizations	0 Demand Deposits
Financial Organizations	1 Savings Deposits and Interest
Savings and Loans	2 Money orders and Travelers Checks
Business Associations	3 Drafts, Certified Checks, Christmas Club Checks, Cashier Checks
Title Companies-Escrow	
Escrow Companies	
Collection Agencies	4 Contents of Safe Deposit BOxes and Safekeeping Items
Credit Bureaus	
	5 Trust Deposits (Escrow)
Convalescent Homes	6 Liquidating Funds
Mortgage Companies	7 Earnings due shareholders-Dividends
Equity & Morgtage	8 Shares of Stock
	9 Miscellaneous Funds-(Wages, Refunds, Accounts Payable, Collections, etc.)
Life Insurance Companies	1 Matured or Terminated Policies
	2 Policy Holders Dividends
	3 Premium Refunds Returned
	6 Liquidating Funds
	7 Earnings due Shareholders
	8 Unclaimed Shares Stock
	9 Miscellaneous Funds-(Commissions, Wages, Accounts Payable, etc.)
Public Officer and Agencies Other Holders, Courts, etc.	9 All Intangible Personal Property
Utilities:	5 Trust Deposits (Escrow)
Telephone	6 Liquidating Funds
Water	7 Earnings due Shareholders
Electric	8 Shares of Stock
Natural Gas	9 Miscellaneous Funds-(Wages, Refunds Accounts Payable, Collections, etc.)
Insurance Companies (Other than Life Insurance)	1 Terminated Policies
	2 Policyholders Dividends
	3 Premium Refund Returned
	6 Liquidating Funds
	7 Earnings due Shareholders
	8 Unclaimed Shares of Stock
	9 Miscellaneous Funds-(Commissions, Wages, Accounts Payable, etc.)
Credit Unions	1 Savings Deposits and Interest
Loan Companies	2 Money Orders and Travelers Checks
Credit Associations	3 Drafts, Certified Checks, Christmas Club Checks, Cashier Checks
	6 Liquidating Funds
	9 Miscellaneous Funds

Different types of intangible unclaimed property.

son. There is an advantage to doing this — you won't be denied access to the list. This is your privilege.

This happened in Connecticut. A 14-year-old boy was having trouble getting the list from his state's office, so he went in person. He reviewed the list, jotted down 30 names, and began his search for the rightful owners. After finding the first few names on the list, he told me that he's now $16,212 richer — and he earned his wealth in just a few days.

Here are the names, addresses and numbers of the state agencies to contact.

State Offices Of Unclaimed Property

ALABAMA
Unclaimed Property Division
Revenue Department
206 Adminstration Building
Montgomery, Alabama 36130
205/261-3369

ALASKA
Unclaimed Property Division
Revenue Department
State Office Building
Pouch S A
Juneau, Alaska 99811
907/465-2322

ARIZONA
Unclaimed Property Division
Revenue Department
Capitol Building
1700 W. Washington Street
Phoenix, Arizona 85007
602/255-4425

ARKANSAS
Unclaimed Property Division
Finance & Administration Dept.
DFA Building
Little Rock, Arkansas 72203
501/371-1458

CALIFORNIA
Unclaimed Property Division
Controller Office
PO Box 1019
State Capitol Building
Sacramento, California 95804
916/322-4166

COLORADO
Unclaimed Property Division
Revenue Department
140 State Capitol
Denver, Colorado 80203
303/866-2441

CONNECTICUT
Unclaimed Property Division
Tax Department
20 Trinity Street
Hartford, Connecticut 06106
203/566-5516

DELAWARE
Unclaimed Property Division
Treasury Department
Thomas Collins Building
Wilmington, Delaware 19801
302/736-4208

FLORIDA
Unclaimed Property Division

Revenue Department
1401 The Capitol
Tallahassee, Florida 32301
904/487-2583

GEORGIA
Unclaimed Property Division
Revenue Department
405 Trinity-Washington Building
270 Washington Street S. W.
Atlanta, Georgia 30334
404/656-4244

HAWAII
Unclaimed Property Division
Taxation Department
425 Queen Street
Honolulu, Hawaii 96813
808/548-7650

IDAHO
Department of Revenue and Taxation
State Tax Commission
PO Box 56
Boise, Idaho 83756
208/334-4516

ILLINOIS
Unclaimed Property Division
Revenue Department
11th & Ash Street
Springfield, Illinois 62708
217/782-5552

INDIANA
Unclaimed Property Division
Revenue Department
State Office Building #1022

Indianapolis, Indiana 46204
317/232-6348

IOWA
Unclaimed Property Division
Revenue Department
Hoover Building
10th Street
Des Moines, Iowa 50319
515/281-5540

KANSAS
Unclaimed Property Division
Revenue Department
State Office Building
535 Kansas Avenue
Box 737
PO Box 1517
Topeka, Kansas 66601
913/296-2031

KENTUCKY
Unclaimed Property Division
Treasury Department
Capitol Annex
Frankfort, Kentucky 40620
502/564-2100

LOUISIANA
Unclaimed Property Division
Revenue & Taxation Department
PO Box 201
300 N. Ardenwood Drive
Baton Rouge, Louisiana 70804
504/925-7424

MAINE
Unclaimed Property Division

Bureau of Taxation
State Office Building
Augusta, Maine 04333
207/289-2771

MARYLAND
Unclaimed Property Division
Comptroller of the Treasury
State Treasury Building
Baltimore, Maryland 21201
301/383-4984

MASSACHUSETTS
Unclaimed Property Division
Corportation & Taxation Department
100 Cambridge Street
Boston, Massachussetts 02202
617/727-4201

MICHIGAN
Unclaimed Property Division
Treasury Department
Lansing, Michigan 48922
517/373-0550

MINNESOTA
Unclaimed Property Division
Revenue Department
Centennial Office Building
St. Paul, Minnesota 55155
612/296-2568

MISSISSIPPI
Unclaimed Property Division
Tax Commission
102 Woolfolk Building
Jackson, Mississippi 39205
601/354-7117

MISSOURI
Unclaimed Property Division
Revenue Department
227 State Capitol
PO Box 210
Jefferson Building
Jefferson City, Missouri 65102
314/751-2096

MONTANA
Unclaimed Property Division
Revenue Department
Sam W. Mitchell Building
Helena, Montana 59620
406/444-2460

NEBRASKA
Unclaimed Property Division
Revenue Department
PO Box 94788
Lincoln, Nebraska 68509
402/471-2455

NEVADA
Unclaimed Property Division
Treasury Department
Capitol Building
Carson City, Nevada 89710
702/885-5200

NEW HAMPSHIRE
Unclaimed Property Division
Taxation Board
19 Pillsbury Street
Concord, New Hampshire 03301
613/271-2621

NEW JERSEY
Unclaimed Property Division
Divison of Taxation
W. State & Willow Street
Trenton, New Jersey 08625
609/292-4827

NEW MEXICO
Unclaimed Property Division
Taxation & Revenue Department
Manuel Lujan Building
PO Box 30
Santa Fe, New Mexico 87509-0630
505/988-2290

NEW YORK
Unclaimed Property Division
Tax & Finance Department
Campus Tax & Finance Building
Albany, New York 12227
518/457-2902

NORTH CAROLINA
100 Albemarle Building
325 N. Salisbury Street
Raleigh, NC 27611
919/733-4440

NORTH DAKOTA
Unclaimed Property Division
Tax Department
Capitol Building
Bismark, North Dakota 58505
701/224-2806

OHIO
Unclaimed Property Division
Taxation Department

30 E. Broad Street
Columbus, Ohio 43215
614/466-4433

OKLAHOMA
Unclaimed Property Division
Tax Commission
2501 Lincoln Boulevard
Oklahoma City, Oklahoma 73194
405/521-3237

OREGON
Unclaimed Property Division
Treasury Department
1445 State Street
State Capitol Building
Salem, Oregon 97310
503/378-3806

PENNSYLVANIA
Unclaimed Property Division
Revenue Department
Strawberry Square
Harrisburg, Pennsylvania 17127
717/787-6960

RHODE ISLAND
Unclaimed Property Division
Tax Department
289 Promenade Street
Providence, Rhode Island 02908
401/277-2905

SOUTH CAROLINA
Unclaimed Property Division
Tax Commission
Calhoun Office Building
Columbia, South Carolina 29214

803/758-2196

SOUTH DAKOTA
Unclaimed Property Division
Revenue Department
Kneip Building
Pierre, South Dakota 57501
605/773-3378

TENNESSEE
Unclaimed Property Division
Andrew Jackson Building
Nashville, Tennessee 37219
615/741-6499

TEXAS
Unclaimed Property Division
Revenue Department
111 E. 17th Street
Austin, Texas 78701
512/475-2086

UTAH
Unclaimed Property Division
Tax Commission
219 State Capitol
Salt Lake City, Utah 84114
801/533-7183

VERMONT
Unclaimed Property Division
Tax Department
109 State Street
Montpelier, Vermont 05602
802/828-2301

VIRGINIA
Unclaimed Property Division

State Treasurer's Office
PO Box 6-H
Richmond, Virginia 23207
804/225-2393

WASHINGTON
Unclaimed Property Division
Revenue Department
General Administration Building
Olympia, Washington 98504
206/754-2630

WEST VIRGINIA
Unclaimed Property Division
Tax Department
W. State Capitol Building
Charleston, West Virginia 25305
304/348-2281

WISCONSIN
Office of State Treasurer
Unclaimed Property Division
PO Box 2114
Madison, Wisconsin 53707
608/267-7977

WYOMING
Unclaimed Property Division
Revenue & Taxation Dept.
State Capitol Building
Cheyenne, Wyoming 82002
307/777-7408

Chapter 3
Business Basics

Now you are on your way to making big money by returning lost money to the rightful owners. Here is how the process works. First, you contact your local state office and get a list of unclaimed property owners. The state office can give you a list of all unclaimed owners or they can direct you to a newspaper publishing of current unclaimed property owners. This chapter contains one newspaper clipping of unclaimed owners.

After you find a particular individual you contact him or her either by phone or by mail. You would then explain to this person that you can send a check for an amount (which you will specify) if he or she signs the contract you are sending. After the person signs the contract, you will then get your share of his or her unclaimed money. Easy, isn't it?

Now that you have the list of names from your state office, I will help you out by giving you some business tips. The first question is: how much should you charge for your finder's fee? I say that one-third or 33.3 percent of a share of the unclaimed money is fair. There are those who charge up to 65 percent commission to find owners of unclaimed money. I think that is rather high. But the ball is in your court — you can charge whatever you think is fair. However, some states do have limits to the amount of fee you can charge.

Gall, Brenda Humstone, Address Unknown
Gallegos, Luigi, 148-27 61st Rd., Flushing, NY
Garner, Charles E., Add. Ukn.
Gavin, Audrey c/o Philip Gavin, Esq., 104-26 Jamaica Avenue, Richmond Hill, NY 11418
Gene Frankel Theatre Workshop Inc. (The), Address Unknown
German, Emilio & Giovanna German, Wavecrest Drive, Mastic Beach, NY 11951
Gerodias, Maurine Assoc. Inc., Address Unknown
Giampontzef, Irene, 3 Box 268, Farmingdale, NJ 07727
Gibson, Mamie L., Address Ukn.
Gilbert, Timothy A., Add. Ukn.
Giordano, Linda A., 2044 21st Dr., Brooklyn, NY 11214
Gislason, Kristjan, 4218 Sonnierlok, Toledo, Ohio 43606
Gittens, Marjorie, 172-12 71st Ave., Flushing, NY 11365
Gladden, Earle, Address Ukn.
Glenmore Chrome Co., 157-16 Northern Blvd., Flushing, NY 11358
Gleitsman, Rael, P.O. Box 14, Foster Center, Rhode Island
Glenwood Fabrics, 80 Beckwith Ave., Patterson, NJ 07502
Global Aquatics Ltd., 1419 Neck Road, Brooklyn, NY 11229
Globe Motor Car Co., 1230 Bloomfield Ave., Fairfield. NJ 07006
Globus, Helen, Address Unknown
Goings, Alvin, Address Unknown
Gold Seal Vinemards, Add. Ukn.
Gold, Sonia. 2340 Linwood Ave., Fort Lee, NJ 07024
Golden, Riva L., Address Ukn.
Goldfarb. Morton M. D., Address Unknown
Gonzales, John, Address Unknown
Gonzalez, Antonio, Address Ukn.
Gordon, Dennis, 170 Varick St., New York, NY
Gordon, T. John, Address Ukn.
Goresiglio, Gertrude G., Address Unknown
Govatzidaki, Sofia, 33 Bayville Ave., Bayville, NY 11709
Granados, Pedro. 1443 Hildala Courtlepland, Cal. 91786
Great Adventure Inc., 320 E. 65th Street, New York, NY 10021
Great Eastern Linens, 25 Saddle River, Garfield, NJ 07026
Green, Anne E., 140-26 184 St., Springfield Gardens, NY
Greene. Jimmi. 90 Manor Dr., Great Neck, NY
Gropper, Fred. Address Unknown
Grosch. David L., 742 W. Bristol, Elkhart, Ind. 46514
Grossman, Nathan, 52 East 52nd St., Brooklyn, NY 11212
Grumapple Cafe Inc., 628 W. 52nd St.. New York, NY 10019
Grune & Stratton, 111 Fifth Ave., New York, NY 10003
Guill, John, Address Unknown
Gutierrez, Jose F., Address Ukn.
Guzman, Carlos, Address Ukn.
H. F. D. Inc., Linden Plaza, 1111 W. St. Georges Ave., Linden, NJ 07036
Kristen, James, 893 Brooklyn Ave., Brooklyn, NY 11203
Krusher, Henry L. Foundation Inc., 25 W. 43rd St., NY 10036
Kunzig, Richard J., Add. Ukn.
Lack, Dorothy, Address Unknown
Ladies Aux of Prophet Elizah, American Orthodox Catholic Church-Bingo, 1610 Lexington Avenue, New York, NY
Lady Fair, 510 Franklin Avenue, Nutley, NJ 07110
Lady Vivian of The Village, 101 West 12th St., New York, NY
Laird, Bissell & Meeds Inc., Address Unknown
Lambray Maureen, Inc., Address Unknown
Larkin, Estelle E., 44 Rockelle St., Staten Island, New York
Laschener, Irving, 50 Brighton 1 Rd., Brooklyn, NY 11235
Laspada, E., Address Unknown
Laurel Lamp Mfg. Co., Address Unknown
Layanconpanion, Thomas, Address Unknown
Leavin, Gabrielle, Address Ukn.
Leddy, Mary B., Address Ukn.
Leeds, Grace L., Address Ukn.
Leiberman, John, Address Ukn.
Lerman, Rose, Address Unknown
Lesher, Maryon, Address Ukn.
Lessman, Lieschotte, Add. Ukn.
Levenson, Frances, 420 Central Park W., New York, NY 10025
Levesque, O'Rula, Address Ukn.
Lewie, Marjorie, 18-65 211th Ave., Bayside. NY 11360
Lezette, Richard, Address Ukn.
Liberty Travel, 135 West 41st, New York, NY
Lichter, Norman, Coin Process Center, 7425 Cirrack
Lilltizoh, Robert F., 250 W. 135th Street
Lin, Ryun Hee, c/o Mr. Hinder, 619 Sadler Street, Aberdeen, Maryland
Linen, Jahathan Scrantan, Address Unknown
Loews Clearing Corp., Hotels Tenant, Address Unknown
Lofton, Douglas, 757 Schnenk Avenue, Brooklyn, NY 11207
Lotaripe, Donald, 1920 McGraw Avenue
Loveman, Mr. & Mrs., Add. Ukn.
Lumadue. Charles R., Add. Ukn.
Lurey Alpha Hairdressers, Inc., 490 Sixth Ave., New York, NY 10011
Lynch R. J. Co., 24 William Street, Staten Island, NY 10304
M.P. Card & Book Shops, Inc., Spruce St., Ramsey, NJ 07446
MacDonald. Lorraine M., Address Unknown
Mack, Adele F., Address Ukn.
Mac Kinnon, William. Add. Ukn.
Mahoney, J. & J. Address Ukn.
Mammon, Jack, 4206 12th Ave.
Mams. Hannah Shirley, 876 East 223rd Street. Bronx, NY
Mansley, D., Address Unknown
Manway, Damar, c/o Manway Construcion Co., 161-10 Jamaica Ave., Jam., NY 11432
Parish Securities Corp., Address Unknown
Parker, Edward O., 120-16 172nd Street, Jamaica, NY 11434
Parkes, Alice, 1429 Carroll Street, Brooklyn, NY 11213
Párotta, Joseph D., Address Ukn.
Paschetto, Robert W. / Cecilia, 130-07 59th Ave., Flushing, NY
Pascuiti, Pearl, 2166 Allan Ave., Yorktown Heights, NY 10598
Passalasqua, Deborah, Add. Ukn.
Patterson, Ethel, 200 Cozine St., Brooklyn, NY 11207
Patterson, Gussie A., 2160 Seward Avenue. Bronx, New York
Paulino, Romulo Miguel, Address Unknown
Pelletiere, Sal, Address Unknown
Penjola, C., Address Unknown
Peracasa, Veronica, Hotel Pierre, 5th Ave. & 61st St., New York, NY
Perez, Esther, 112-44 197th St., Hollis, NY 11412
Perez, Francisco, 89-15 Parsons Blvd., Jamaica, NY 11432
Pergament, Penny, Address Ukn.
Perkins, D. L., Address Unknown
Perlez, J., A.P.A., 13 East 10th St., NY
Permanent Mission of Guinea to U.N., United Nations, New York, NY
Perry, Harold C., Address Ukn.
Persepolis Chartering, Add. Ukn.
Pester, Goldberg & Schiff, Address Unknown
Phillips, Arthur L., Add. Ukn.
Phoenix Shipping Co. Inc., 105 Washington St., New York
Pickeus, Lon, Address Unknown
Pierce, Bruce, 701 Cleveland St., Brooklyn, NY 11208
Pierro, Gloria, 33-34th St., Brooklyn, NY
Pilgrim Baptist Cathedral (The), Address Unknown
Pine Rd. Estates Corp., Add. Ukn.
Piscapo, A. B., 16 Lake Gilead Rd., Carmel, NY 10512
Pitgairn, William S., Add. Ukn.
Piton, Jacqueline AnneMarie, 223-46 112th Rd., Queens Village, New York 11429
Pittman, David L., 1 Christopher St.
Pizzaro, Eugenia L., Add. Ukn.
Platt, Ronald L., Address Ukn.
Pleshette, Norman, Add. Ukn.
Ploss, Leon, Address Uknown
Pool, Priscilla, Address Unknown
Porcu, Joseph J., Address Ukn.
Porcu, Rose A., Address Ukn.
Pres, Karl Preuss, 283 Medford Ave., Patchogue, NY 11772
Priggen Photography Inc., Address Unknown
Promenade Cafe, Rock. Center, NY 10017
Prophet Elizah American Ort. Catholic Church Sp. Bingo, 1610 Lex. Ave., New York, NY
Protection Ins. Agcy Inc., Address Unknown
Puccino, Roslyn, 245-38 149th Ave., Rosedale, NY 11422
Pummer, Mendel, Address Ukn.
Quigley, Donald F., Add. Ukn.

New York newspaper publishing of unclaimed property owners.

Some states won't allow you to share one-third with the property owner you've found. If this is true in your state, I know of a way you can still get the fee you deserve. Instead of agreeing with the property owner that you'll share one-third of the property, draw up an agreement saying that the person you've found will give you a set fee. You charge the person for your time and expenses it cost you to locate him or her.

I suggest that you ask a lawyer or someone who is competent in the legal profession to help you, since your fee is the most important part of this business! When you draw up the contract between you (the Investigator) and the unclaimed property owner (the Claimant), be sure to include a separate fee for your services. I have included a guideline for drawing up the contract between you and the unclaimed property owner. Be sure you check with a lawyer first to make sure everything in your contract is legal — as you know, each state is different.

Once you have the names, the next step is contacting the person. Here is a sample conversation for you to study. In my experience of contacting unclaimed property owners, this is how a typical conversation would go:

You: May I speak to Mr. John Doe?

John: Hello. This is he.

You: Hello, Mr. Doe. This is Tom Peters with People Finders here in San Diego.

John: What can I do for you?

You: We have come across $36,000 that we have assisted in obtaining for you.

John: Wait a minute, I don't have $36,000 coming to me.

You: Mr. Doe, haven't you heard of wealthy people leaving money behind to people that didn't even know them?

John: Yes.

You: Well, Mr. Doe, this money is definitely yours; however, I can't tell you the source of this money at this point.

John: Are you telling me the truth? Is this some type of crank?

You: I assure you, Mr. Doe, that everything I am telling you is the complete truth.

John: I could sure use that money. What do I have to do to get it?

You: Mr. Doe, I will be sending you a form in the mail. All you have to do is sign the form and the money is yours.

John: That is all I have to do?

You: Yes, Mr. Doe. Is your correct address 1212 Folly Lane, San Diego, California, 92345?

John: No. It's 7865 Rockherst Street, San Diego, California, 92120.

You: All right. You'll find everything in the form exactly the way I explained it to you. If you have any questions, you're welcome to call me at 567-4564.

John: Okay.

You: Mr. Doe, it is very important that you send this form

back to me as quickly as possible. The sooner I get the form, the sooner you will have your money.

John: Thank you, and I'll be speaking to you soon.

You: You're welcome. Goodbye.

The Contract

After you have found the person and are certain that he is the owner of the unclaimed property, you are now ready to draw up a contract with your attorney. The person you have found will sign the contract, agreeing to pay you either a percentage of the property you have recovered for him, or else the person will agree to pay you a flat fee for your expenses, time, and service. This fee, though, should not be more than 33 percent of the value of the property you recovered for him.

Below is a guideline for the contract between you (the Investigator) and the person whose property you've recovered (the Claimant).

Investigator Agreement/ Contract

Claimant ____________________________________

Address ____________________________________

Reported ____________________________________

Social Security Number ________- ________- ________

Type of Account ____Amount______________________

Stock______________________

I

This agreement is entered into by and between

____

hereinafter referred to as 'Claimant', and

____

hereinafter referred to as 'Investigator.'

II

The Investigator, through his/her efforts, has located Claimant, who will be entitled to the above described assets.

III

Investigator and Claimant do hereby agree that in consideration of Investigator's efforts in locating Claimant and assisting in the actual recovery of the above described assets to which Claimant is entitled, Claimant hereby assigns to the Investigator a set fee of $________________ for expenses and services rendered, providing Claimant recovers described assets.

IV

Investigator and Claimant agree that in the event Claimant is not entitled to assets described above and such assets are not recovered, there is no obligation on either party to the other.

This agreement is void unless executed by both parties.

Investigator ______________________________

Phone________________Address ____________________

____

Date Investigator's Signature

Claimant ______________________________

Phone________________Address ____________________

____

Date Claimant's Signature

It would be a good idea to get the contract looked over by an attorney. Unclaimed property laws change from state to state, so it is important that you abide with the state laws that regulate unclaimed property in your state. The contract in this chapter contains a good guideline for you to follow.

When The Contract Is Returned To You

After you have received the contract returned and signed to you, continue with the next step. You would contact the state unclaimed property office and send them a copy of your signed contract as well as identification (like a Social Security number or drivers license) proving that the person you have found is indeed the person that owns the unclaimed money. Most states do require Social Security, drivers license numbers and other forms of identification.

Make sure you check with your state office to find out exactly what they require of you. When they receive your paperwork, they will send you forms to fill out. After you fill out these forms, they in turn will send a check in the mail. It is as easy as that.

Chapter 4
Tracking Down The Address

Now you have to find these missing people. The list you will receive from the state will give you the full name, address and type of account of people owning unclaimed property. You will now be a private investigator. It's not difficult if you know what to do. In the next few chapters, I will tell you exactly how to find the person or persons you are looking for.

In most cases, these people are no longer living at the address you will receive. But you never know. Send a letter to the address you have on record and see what happens. If someone is living at that address, contact these people and ask them for the whereabouts of the people you are looking for.

How do you find out who is living at that address? You can find the person through the post office, with telephone directories, city directories, plot maps, or the Department of Motor Vehicles (DMV) records. Let's start with the post office.

The Post Office

You may be able to get the address you need through

your local post office. There is a good chance the person you are looking for is no longer at the current address. This doesn't even present a problem if you handle it correctly. The post office has a helpful service for the cost of $1. Ask them for the current address of the person you're searching for. A good idea is to send your letter by registered mail. This will motivate the people at the post office to work on your case sooner. Another idea is to send a letter and write 'DO NOT FORWARD' and 'ADDRESS CORRECTION REQUESTED' on the letter. This second method is not as effective as the first method, but it is free.

Getting a street address from a P.O. box number is tricky. In some cases you may want to reach someone at his or her home address. You can almost always get someone's address with a subpoena. This isn't difficult. Just pay a visit to the county clerk's office and pick up a subpoena form. Type in all the necessary information. Next, you'll need to go to the post office and explain to the clerk that you need the street address of this individual so that you can serve him a subpoena. This should always prove to get you your street address.

Directories

You will probably be able to find the person you are looking for by simply looking through the phone book. If you can't find the person you are looking for in your current phone book, look in older editions of that phone book. Older editions are available in public libraries or the librarians can tell you where you can find old phone books. Don't overlook calling up people with similar surnames of the person you are looking for. You may be surprised how many relatives this person may have in that town. Call up people with similar surnames and ask them first if the person you are looking for resides there. Then ask them if they know of the person you are looking for.

City directories might come in handy, too. They can be of

great assistance to you; they can help you find out who is living at a given address. City directory companies like R. L. Polk and Cole Publications send people door to door to find out who lives at each address. You may find that their directories are more complete than the phone book directories because they even tell you where people with unlisted numbers live. Both of these directories can be found at most public libraries. You may want to look at old city directories. These are available at the Library Of Congress, historical societies or some large public libraries. These books are available at a cost of about $100 a year. If you claim to be with a library that leases the city directories, you can get free information about any address by calling the headquarters of both these city directories. The phone number of R. L. Polk is: (313) 292-3200. The number for Cole Publications is: (402) 475-4591.

Real Estate Plot Maps

Real estate companies have to know who owns every piece of land in this country. No matter what address you find, you will be able to look up the owner on a plot map. These maps are available at your local library or from any real estate agent. If you have a hard time getting these lists, they are available at no cost from your county assesor's office.

Look up the address of the unclaimed owner that you received from the state. On the lot maps you will see the name and address of the owner of the property. The person residing on the property may not necessarily be the owner. He could be renting the address from the owner. Contact the owner either by mail or just look up his phone number and call him. Ask the owner if he is aware of the whereabouts of the person for whom you are searching. He may give you a good lead to follow.

With real estate plot maps you have the ability to look up the person by his address or by his name. Look up the person you are looking for in the town where the person last resided. By doing this, you may be able to find a piece of property that the person owns. If you do find that person, contact him by mail or phone.

The Department of Motor Vehicles offices of some states have a free address verification service that you may use. If you contact them and give them the address, name and date of birth of the person you are looking for, they will tell you if they have the same address in their records. This service is mainly used by car rental agencies. If you want to use this service, use the DMV list I have provided for you in the next few chapters.

Chapter 5
Neighbors, Relatives & Friends

In the previous chapter I showed you how to find someone you are looking for at a particular address. If you are having a hard time locating a certain individual, it's time to ask the neighbors. They could tell you more in less time than you could find out yourself. There are some people who do very little else but watch their neighbors. These are the people you will want to contact. They love telling you everything they know if you approach them the right way. Contact them preferably by phone and ask them what they know about the person you are looking for. Let us review the methods in contacting neighbors and relatives.

1) Use phone books to look up relatives (people with similar last names).

2) Use city directories to look up neighbors and ex-neighbors.

3) Use real estate plot maps to look up neighbors and landlords of neighbors.

Here is how a typical conversation would be between you and one of the neighbors. Let's say the person you are looking for is John Peterson.

You: Hello, Mrs. Smith?

Smith: Yes, speaking.

You: Let me introduce myself. My name is John Doe and I'm with the Acme Financial Company. John Peterson used you as one of his references on his credit application with us. Could I ask you a few questions?

Smith: Sure.

You: How long have you known John Peterson?

Smith: I've known him ever since he moved into this building ... must be about six years.

You: Do you know where Mr. Peterson is employed?

Smith: Last I heard he was a high school teacher at Patrick Henry.

You: Do you know where Mr. Peterson's current address is right now?

Smith: He used to live across the street. He now lives on High Park Lane. Somewhere in the 3900 block.

You: Do you happen to have the exact address?

Smith: Hold on. Here it is. It's 3987 High Park Lane, Apt. 307.

You: One more question, Mrs. Smith. Mr. Peterson has left us 697-4865 as his phone number. Do you list the same phone number?

Smith: That's his old phone number; let me give you his new number. It's 467-9874.

You: I want to thank you for your help. You have been very helpful. Have a good day, Mrs. Smith.

Do you see how many leads Mrs. Smith has given you to the whereabouts of John Peterson? Not only will you know where he lives and works, but you will have his phone number. Using this technique will get you a great deal of information.

You may sense aggressivness when you talk to some people. They may not have liked their old neighbor and would not want to help their old neighbor pass a credit application. If this is the case, tell the person the truth. You may be surprised how much people will help you for your sake and not for their neighbor's sake. If you still have a hard time getting any information from the neighbors, try the delivery man routine.

Go to the neighbor's door in person with a package, addressed to the person you are looking for, in your hands. Make sure the package is personally signed. Let us use John Peterson for this example. Go to the house where John last lived and try to deliver the package. If that person can't help you, go to all the neighbors and ask about John. Explain to the people living there it is an urgent delivery and you must find John. Ask them for a phone number or address. You will be surprised at how helpful neighbors can be. If they don't know very much, ask them for the name and address of a relative or a close friend with whom you could leave the package. One word of caution: do this stunt early or late in the day so that the neighbors are home.

Relatives And Friends

You will find that relatives and friends are more loyal than neighbors. It will be harder to get information from them. I have had success with the credit application story in getting information from relatives and friends. But they ask a lot of questions. You also stand the risk of them not trusting you if you lie to them. If you just want an address, appear at their doorstep with a package. Telling the truth sometimes works if they have a good relationship with the person you are looking for. You will have to use your intuition with friends and relatives for using the best technique. Relatives and good friends are one of the best sources of information you will get, so don't give up on them.

Chapter 6
Drivers Licenses & Automobile Records

Drivers licenses records are public information for anyone. You can obtain them in every state except Arkansas, North Carolina, Pennsylvania and Wisconsin. These records will tell you where a person resides or where he or she was stopped for a moving violation. You can contact any state and find out if that person resides in that state. You may decide to contact the state where your subject applied for his Social Security card. These records will locate the subject for you if he has a driver's license in that state. They will also physically identify the person you are looking for.

When you contact the DMV, ask for a complete list of activities from your subject's driving record. Try to include your subject's full name, date of birth and the required fee.

If a person has transferred his license to another state, it will say so on the license record you will receive. If you can't find your subject, he may have transferred to Texas. Texas is one state that doesn't notify other states of license transfers.

There is one company that can obtain drivers license information for you. It has large data bases that you can access through your computer. You can use this or you can use the list I have provided for you. The choice is yours.

Data Research Inc.
3600 American River Drive
Suite 100
Sacramento, CA 95864

(800) 425-DATA
(916) 485-3282

Here is a complete list of state agencies that will give you drivers license information:

ALABAMA
Drivers License Division
Certification Section
PO Box 1471
Montgomery, Alabama 36102
(205) 832-5100
Fee: $2.00

ALASKA
Department of Public Safety
Drivers License Section
Pouch N
Juneau, Alaska 99801
(907) 465-4396
Fee: $2.00

ARIZONA
Motor Vehicle Department
1801 W. Jefferson Street
Phoenix, Arizona 85007
(602) 255-7011
Fee: Record check — $2.00

ARKANSAS
Office of Driver Services
Traffic Violation Report Unit
PO Box 1272
Little Rock, Arkansas 72203
(501) 371-1671
Fee: $5.00
Write for forms

CALIFORNIA
Department of Motor Vehicles
PO Box 11231
Sacramento, California 95813
(916) 445-4568
Fee: $0.75
Write for forms

COLORADO
Department of Revenue
Motor Vehicle Division
Master File Section
140 W. Sixth Avenue
Denver, Colorado 80204
(303) 892-3407
Fee: $1.25

CONNECTICUT
Department of Motor Vehicles
Copy Record Section

60 State Street
Wethersfield, Connecticut 06109
(203) 566-2638
Fee: $4.00

DELAWARE
Motor Vehicle Department
PO Box 698
Dover, Delaware 19901
(302) 736-4760
Fee: $2.00

DISTRICT OF COLUMBIA
Department of Transportation
Bureau of Motor Vehicles
301 C Street, N.W.
Washington, D.C.
(202) 727-6680
Fee: $0.75

FLORIDA
Drivers License Division
Department of Highway Safety
Kirkham Building
Tallahassee, Florida 32301
(904) 488-9145
Fee: $3.00
Write for forms

GEORGIA
Department of Public Safety
Drivers Service Section
Merit Rating
PO Box 1456
Atlanta, Georgia 30301
(404) 656-2339
Fee: $2.00

HAWAII
District of The First Circuit
Violations Bureau
842 Bethel Street
Honolulu, Hawaii 96813
(808) 548-5735
Fee: $1.00

IDAHO
Department of Law Enforcement
Motor Vehicle Division
PO Box 34
Boise, Idaho 83731
(208) 334-3650
Fee: $1.50

ILLINOIS
Secretary of State
Drivers Services Department
Driver Analysis Section
2701 S. Dirksen Parkway
Springfield, Illinois 62723
(217) 782-3720
Fee: $2.00
Write for forms

INDIANA
Bureau of Motor Vehicles
Paid Mail Section
Room 416, State Office Building
Indianapolis, Indiana 46204
(317) 232-2798
Fee: $1.00

IOWA
Department of Transportation
Records Section

Lucas Building
Des Moines, Iowa 50319
(515) 281-5656
Fee: $1.00

KANSAS
Division of Vehicles
Driver Control Bureau
State Office Building
Topeka, Kansas 66626
(913) 296-3671
Fee: $1.00

KENTUCKY
Division of Driver Licensing
New State Office Building
Frankfort, Kentucky 40601
(502) 564-6800
Fee: $2.00

LOUISIANA
Department of Public Safety
Drivers License Division
O.D.R. Section, Box 1271
Baton Rouge, Louisiana 70821
(504) 925-6343
Fee: $2.00

MAINE
Secretary of State
Motor Vehicle Division
1 Child Street
Augusta, Maine 04333
(207) 289-2761
Fee: $3.00

MASSACHUSETTS
Registry of Motor Vehicles
Court Records Section
100 Nashua Street
Boston, Massachusetts 02114
(617) 727-3842
Fee: $3.00

MICHIGAN
Department of State
Bureau of Driver and Vehicle Services
Commercial Look-Up Unit
7064 Crowner Drive
Lansing, Michigan 48918
(517) 322-1460
Fee: $5.00

MINNESOTA
Department of Public Safety
Drivers License Office
Room 108, State Highway Building
St. Paul, Minnesota 55155
(612) 296-6911
Fee: $2.00
Write for forms

MISSISSIPPI
Mississippi Highway Safety Patrol
Drivers License Issuance Board
PO Box 958
Jackson, Mississippi 39205
(601) 987-1236
Fee: $3.50

MISSOURI
Bureau of Drivers License

Department of Revenue
PO Box 200
Jefferson City, Missouri 65101
(314) 751-4600
Fee: $1.00

MONTANA
Montana Highway Patrol
303 Roberts
Helena, Montana 59601
(406) 449-3000
Fee: $2.00

NEBRASKA
Department of Motor Vehicles
Drivers Record Section
PO Box 94789
Lincoln, Nebraska 68509
(402) 471-2281
Fee: $1.00

NEVADA
CBM of Nevada
Box 1964
Carson City, Nevada 89701
(702) 885-5360
Fee: $1.25

NEW HAMPSHIRE
Division of Motor Vehicles
Driver Record Research Unit
85 Loudon Road
Concord, New Hampshire 03301
(603) 271-2371
Fee: $5.00

NEW JERSEY
Division of Motor Vehicles
Bureau of Security Responsibility
25 S. Montgomery Street
Trenton, New Jersey 08666
(609) 292-7500
Fee: $5.00

NEW MEXICO
Transportation Department
Driver Services Bureau
Manuel Lujan Sr. Building
Santa Fe, New Mexico 87503
(505) 827-7522
Fee: $1.10

NEW YORK
Department of Motor Vehicles
Public Service Bureau
Empire State Plaza
Albany, New York 12228
(518) 473-5595
Fee: $2.00

NORTH CAROLINA
Traffic Records Section
Division of Motor Vehicles
Raleigh, North Carolina 27611
(919) 733-4241
Fee: $1.00
Write for forms

NORTH DAKOTA
Drivers License Division
Capitol Grounds
Bismarck, North Dakota 58505

(701) 224-2600
Fee: $2.00

OHIO
Bureau of Motor Vehicles
PO Box 16520
Columbus, Ohio 43216
(614) 863-7500
Fee: $1.00

OKLAHOMA
Driver Records Service
Department of Public Safety
PO Box 11415
Oklahoma City, Oklahoma 73136
(405) 424-4011
Fee: $3.00

OREGON
Motor Vehicles Division
1905 Lona Avenue
Salem, Oregon 97314
(503) 371-2200
Fee: $6.00

PENNSYLVANIA
Department of Transportation
Bureau of Accident Analysis
Operator Information Section
Room 212
Transportation and Safety Building
Harrisburg, Pennsylvania 17120
(717) 783-6605
Fee: $1.50
Write for required form

RHODE ISLAND
Registry of Motor Vehicles
Room 101G
State Office Building
Providence, Rhode Island 02903
(401) 277-2970
Fee: $1.50

SOUTH CAROLINA
Department of Highways and Public Transportation
Driver Record Check Section, Room 201
Columbia, South Carolina 29216
(605) 758-2125
Fee: $3.00
Write for forms

SOUTH DAKOTA
Department of Public Safety
Driver Improvement Program
118 W. Capitol
Pierce, South Dakota 57501
(605) 773-3191
Fee: $2.00
Write for forms

TENNESSEE
Department of Safety
Jackson Building
Nashville, Tennessee 37219
(615) 741-3954
Fee: $3.00

TEXAS
Department of Public Safety
License of Issuance and Driver Records
PO Box 4087

Austin, Texas 78773
(512) 465-2000
Fee: $1.00
Write for forms

UTAH
Drivers License Division
314 State Office Building
Salt Lake City, Utah 84114
(801) 965-4400
Fee: $1.00

VERMONT
Agency of Transportation
Department of Motor Vehicles
Montpelier, Vermont 05602
(802) 828-2121
Fee: $3.00

VIRGINIA
Division of Motor Vehicles
Driver Licensing and Information Department
PO Box 27412
Richmond, Virginia 23269
(804) 257-0538
Fee: $3.00

WASHINGTON
Division of Licensing
Department of Motor Vehicles
Olympia, Washington 98501
(206) 753-6969
Fee: $1.50

WEST VIRGINIA
Driver Improvement Division

Department of Motor Vehicles
1800 Washington Street, East
Charleston, West Virginia 25305
(304) 348-3900
Fee: $1.00

WISCONSIN
Department of Transportation
Driver Record File
PO Box 7918
Madison, Wisconsin 53707
(608) 266-2261
Fee: $1.00
Write for forms

WYOMING
Department of Revenue
2200 Carey Avenue
Cheyenne, Wyoming 82001
(307) 777-6516
Fee: $1.00

License Plates

It is always handy to be able to know who owns which car. In your attempt to locate an owner of unclaimed property you may be able to use license plate information. You may find a car at your subject's address that may be able to give you information. These are, however, circumstances where you would want to speak to an owner of a car. I have included state agencies to contact for car ownership information. This information is available in every state. Here is a complete list of state license plate offices:

ALABAMA
Motor Vehicle and Licensing Division
PO Box 104

3030 E. Boulevard
Montgomery, Alabama 36130
Fee: $0.25

ARKANSAS
Motor Vehicle Division
PO Box 1272
Little Rock, Arkansas 72203
Fee: $1.00

ALASKA
Division of Motor Vehicles
PO Box 960
Anchorage, Alaska 99510
Fee: $2.00

ARIZONA
Arizona Motor Vehicle Division
PO Box 2100
Phoenix, Arizona 85001
Fee: $1.00

CALIFORNIA
Department of Motor Vehicles
PO Box 11231
Sacramento, California 95813
Fee: $1.00

COLORADO
Department of Revenue
Motor Vehicle Master Files Section
140 W. 6th Avenue
Denver, Colorado 80204
Fee: $1.25

CONNECTICUT
Commissioner of Motor Vehicles

60 State Street
Wethersfield, Connecticut 06109
Fee: $1.00

DELAWARE
Motor Vehicle Division
Registration Section
PO Box 698
Dover, Delaware 19901
Fee: $2.00

DISTRICT OF COLUMBIA
Bureau of Motor Vehicles
301 C Street, N.W.
Washington, D.C. 20001
Fee: $0.50

FLORIDA
Department of Highway Safety and Motor Vehicles
Kirkman Building
Tallahassee, Florida 32301
Fee: $0.50

GEORGIA
Department of Revenue
Motor Vehicle Division
Trinity Washington Building
Atlanta, Georgia 30334
Fee: $0.50

HAWAII
Director of Finance
County of Hawaii
25 Apuni Street
Hilo, Hawaii 96720

Director of Finance
County of Kauai
Lihue, Hawaii 06766

Director of Finance
County of Maui
Wailuku, Maui 96793

Director fo Finance
County of Honolulu
1455 S. Bertania
Honolulu, Hawaii 96814

IDAHO
Motor Vehicle Division
Department of Law Enforcement
PO Box 34
Boise, Idaho 83731
Fee: $1.50

ILLINOIS
Secretary of State
2701 S. Dirksen Parkway
Springfield, Illinois 62756
Fee: $2.00

INDIANA
Bureau of Motor Vehicles, Room 314
State Office Building
Indianapolis, Indiana 46204
Fee: $1.00

IOWA
Department of Transportation
Office of Vehicle Registration
Lucas Building

Des Moines, Iowa 50319
Fee: $1.00

KANSAS
Division of Vehicles
Department of Revenue
State Office Building
Topeka, Kansas 66626
Fee: $1.00

KENTUCKY
Department of Justice
Bureau of State Police
State Office Building
Frankfort, Kentucky 40601
Fee: $1.00

LOUISIANA
Department of Public Safety
Vehicle Regulation Division
PO Box 66196
Baton Rouge, Louisiana 70896
Fee: $2.00

MAINE
Motor Vehicle Division
1 Child Street
Augusta, Maine 04333
Fee: $2.00

MARYLAND
Motor Vehicle Administration
6601 Richie Highway N.E.
Glen Burnie, Maryland 21062
Fee: $1.00

MASSACHUSETTS
Registry of Motor Vehicles
100 Nashua Street
Boston, Massachusetts 02114
Fee: $1.50

MICHIGAN
Department of State
Bureau of Driver and Vehicle Services
7064 Crowner Drive
Lansing, Michigan 48918
Fee: $4.00

MINNESOTA
Driver and Vehicle Services
Transportation Building
St. Paul, Minnesota 55155
Fee: $1.00

MISSISSIPPI
Motor Vehicle Comptroller
PO Box 1140
Jackson, Mississippi 39205
Fee: $1.00

MISSOURI
Department of Revenue
Motor Vehicle and Drivers Licensing Bureau
Jefferson City, Missouri 65101
Fee: $1.00

MONTANA
Department of Justice
Registrars Bureau
Motor Vehicle Division
Deer Lodge, Montana 59722
Fee: $2.00

NEBRASKA
Administrator of Titles and Registration
Department of Motor Vehicles
Capitol Building
Lincoln, Nebraska 68509
Fee: $1.00

NEVADA
Department of Motor Vehicles
555 Wright Way
Carson City, Nevada 89711
Fee: $1.50

NEW HAMPSHIRE
Motor Vehicles Division
85 Loudon Road
Concord, New Hampshire 03301
Fee: $3.50

NEW JERSEY
Division of Motor Vehicles
Bureau of Office Services
Certified Information Unit
25 South Montgomery Street
Trenton, New Jersey 08666
Fee: $5.00

NEW MEXICO
Motor Vehicle Division
Manual Lujan Sr. Building
Santa Fe, New Mexico 87503
Fee: $1.10

NEW YORK
Motor Vehicle Department
Registration Records Section
Empire State Plaza
Albany, New York 12228
Fee: $2.00

NORTH CAROLINA
Division of Motor Vehicles
Motor Vehicle Building
1100 New Bern Avenue
Raleigh, North Carolina 27611
Fee: $0.50

NORTH DAKOTA
Motor Vehicle Department
State Office Building
9th and Boulevard
Bismarck, North Dakota 58505
Fee: $0.50
Write for forms

OHIO
Bureau of Motor Vehicles
Correspondence Section MVVRRC
PO Box 16520
Columbus, Ohio 43216
Fee: $0.50

OKLAHOMA
Oklahoma Tax Commission
Motor Vehicle Division
2501 N. Lincoln Boulevard
Oklahoma City, Oklahoma 73194
Fee: $1.00

OREGON
Motor Vehicle Division
1905 Lana Aveue, N.E.
Salem, Oregon 97314
Fee: $1.00

PENNSYLVANIA
Department of Transportation
Motor Vehicle Bureau
Harrisburg, Pennsylvania 17122
Fee: $2.50

RHODE ISLAND
Registry of Motor Vehicles
State Office Building
Providence, Rhode Island 02903
Fee: $1.00

SOUTH CAROLINA
Department of Highways Public Transportation
Motor Vehicle Division
PO Box 1498
Columbia, South Carolina 29216
Fee: $1.00

SOUTH DAKOTA
Department of Public Safety
Division of Motor Vehicles
118 West Capitol
Pierre, South Dakota 57501

TENNESSEE
Motor Vehicle Division
Information Unit
Jackson Building

Nashville, Tennessee 37242
Fee: $0.50

TEXAS
Department of Highways and Public Transportation
Motor Vehicle Division
40th and Jackson
Austin, Texas 78779
Fee: $0.25

UTAH
Motor Vehicle Department
1095 Motor Avenue
Salt Lake City, Utah 84116
Fee: $1.50

VERMONT
Department of Motor Vehicles
Montpelier, Vermont 05603
Fee: $1.50

VIRGINIA
Division of Motor Vehicles
Box 27412
Richmond, Virginia 23269
Fee: $3.00

WASHINGTON
Vehicle Records
Department of Licensing
PO Box 9909
Olympia, Washington 98504
Fee: $2.00

WEST VIRGINIA
Division of Motor Vehicles

1800 Washington Street E.
Charleston, West Virginia 25305
Fee: $0.25
Correspond on business letterhead

WISCONSIN
Vehicle Files
Department of Transportation
PO Box 7909
Madison, Wisconsin 53707
Fee: $1.00

WYOMING
Motor Vehicle Division
2200 Carey Avenue
Cheyenne, Wyoming 82002
Fee: $1.00

Chapter 7

Get The Government To Help You

There is a wealth of information at your local county courthouse. You may be able to find the person you are looking for at the county courthouse. All of the information at the courthouse is supposed to be public information. Ask the clerk at the desk for a file on the person you are looking for. Look through the file and look to see what address was used. In some cases people use different addresses when they are served a citation than the address on their drivers license.

Sometimes the clerk behind the desk may deny you the information you want. According to your state's 'Freedom of Information Act' he should give you the information you request. If he gives you a hard time, point out the freedom act to this hard-nose employee. If you feel you are getting nowhere, ask for his supervisor and keep on arguing. They usually give in and give you want you want. You must be persistent.

There is always the possibility that the person you are looking for has passed away. In this case you would want to know that this person has indeed died. Obituary records are kept at the county clerk's office. If you use the county clerk's office, you must be sure that the person's last known address was in that county. Records are kept from county to county.

Social Security Records

The Social Security department can practically reach everybody in the United States. These records can tell you anything you want to know about an individual. The only way you can get someone's records is if you knew someone who worked for the Social Security department. The department is always behind on its records about two to four months.

The Social Security department has one division that will help you out. This division will let you send a letter to any person. They will not give you the address of that person; they will just forward your letter. This comes in really handy so that you could contact a person who owns unclaimed money by mail. Include your phone number and address so that this person can contact you. Get the person excited about the money he will receive and be very honest with him. When you write to the Social Security department, try to include as much information as you can about the person you are looking for. The address of the division that will forward your letters is: Social Security Administration, Location Services, 6401 Security Blvd., Baltimore, Maryland, 21235.

If you have the Social Security number of the person you are looking for, you may be able to use this prefix. By prefix I mean the first three numbers of a Social Security number. This prefix will show you where this person is from. Sometimes people go back to the state they came from. If a person last resided in Kansas and his Social Security number is from New York, this person may be living in New York.

001-003 NEW HAMPSHIRE
004-007 MAINE
008-009 VERMONT
010-034 MASSACHUSETTS
035-039 RHODE ISLAND
040-049 CONNECTICUT
050-134 NEW YORK
135-158 NEW JERSEY
159-211 PENNSYLVANIA
212-220 MARYLAND
221-222 DELAWARE
223-231 VIRGINIA
232-236 WEST VIRGINIA
237-246 NORTH CAROLINA
247-251 SOUTH CAROLINA
252-260 GEORGIA
261-267 FLORIDA
268-302 OHIO
303-317 INDIANA
318-361 ILLINOIS
362-386 MICHIGAN
387-399 WISCONSIN
400-407 KENTUCKY
408-415 TENNESSEE
416-424 ALABAMA
425-428 MISSISSIPPI
429-432 ARKANSAS
433-439 LOUISIANA
440-448 OKLAHOMA
449-467 TEXAS
468-477 MINNESOTA
478-485 IOWA
486-500 MISSOURI
501-502 NORTH DAKOTA
503-504 SOUTH DAKOTA
505-508 NEBRASKA

509-515 KANSAS
516-517 MONTANA
518-519 IDAHO
520 WYOMING
521-524 COLORADO
525 NEW MEXICO
526-527 ARIZONA
528-529 UTAH
530 NEVADA
531-539 WASHINGTON
540-544 OREGON
545-573 CALIFORNIA
574 ALASKA
575-576 HAWAII
577-579 DISTRICT OF COLUMBIA

Military People

If you know that the person you want to reach is in the service — you are in luck. There is a department in the military that will locate a person in the service for you. Just send the person's full name as well as his or her Social Security number with $2.85 to: World Wide Locator, Fort Benjamin Harrison, IN 46216. They will write you a letter telling where the person you are looking for is stationed.

Chapter 8
Other Methods Of Locating People

Credit bureaus can help you to locate an individual. Many of their financial transactions are in their reports. In some cases you may not get an exact address but will be able to find out where they are located. Once you find out their approximate location finding their address is easy. Most credit bureaus are not a good resource of information. The two best ones are TRW and Trans-World. Anyone can get information from these bureaus. You just have to be a business and pay their $50 a year fee.

Credit Card Companies

Credit card companies can help you find the person you are looking for. If you know the person you are looking for has a credit card and you know his credit card number, you will be able to get his current address. Watch how you would find an address. Let us say that you are looking for John Peterson and you have his credit card number.

Operator: Acme Credit Deparment, may I help you?

You: You haven't been sending me my statements.

Operator: What is your account number and name?

You: My name is John Peterson and my account number is 45-0098-0987.

Operator: You say you haven't been receiving your statements?

You: Yes, can you tell me to what address you have been sending my statements?

Operator: We have been sending your statements to 1265 Tower Rd. San Diego, CA 92119.

You: That seems to be okay. How much do I owe you?

Operator: You have an outstanding balance of $176.98. Would you like me to send you another statement?

You: Yes, and I want to thank you for your help.

The Salvation Army

Many transients have been known to carry hundreds of thousands of dollars in their possessions. One transient that was found frozen to death in Montana had about $75,000 in bonds and securities in a plastic bag he carried with him. The person you are looking for might be a transient.

The Salvation Army operates many missions all over this country. If you have reason to believe that the person you are looking for is a transient, you may want to ask the Salvation Army for help. Remember that finding people is really not their specialty, though. They have three different offices. Contact the office that you would feel would help you the most.

Eastern Headquarters: (for states CT, DE, ME, MA, NH, NJ, NY, OH, PA, VT and RI) Write: Salvation Army Missing

Person's Service, 120 West 14th St., New York, NY 10010.

Central Headquarters: (for states IL, IN, IA, KS, MI, MN, MO, NE, ND, SD and WI) Write: Salvation Army Missing Person's Service, 860 Dearborne St., Chicago, IL 60610.

Western Headquarters: (for states AK, AZ, CA, CO, HI, ID, MT, NY, NM, UT, WA and WY.) Write: Salvation Army Missing Person's Service, 30840 Hawthorne Blvd., Rancho Palos Verdes, CA 90274.

Southern Headquarters: (for states AL, AR, FL, GA, KY, LA, MD, MS, NC, OK, SC, TN, TX, VA, DC and WV) Write: Salvation Army Missing Person's Service, 1424 N.E. Expressway, Atlanta, GA 30329.

Chapter 9
The Money Could Be Yours

You may own unclaimed money. One out of ten people has lost money. You may be one of those people or an heir to one of those people. People that die almost always leave some money behind. You may possibly be the heir to thousands and not even know it. You can receive your money by following these simple steps. Answer the following questions, you may have money waiting for you. You may be very surprised at how much money can be yours.

1) Have you been married or divorced?
2) Changed jobs?
3) Changed your name?
4) Moved in the past 15 years?
5) Retired?
6) Had a safe-deposit box?
7) Had a death in your family or someone related to you?
8) Bought stocks, bonds or any type of a security?
9) Worked for a city, state, county or federal government office?
10) Worked for the railroad?
11) Served with any division of the armed forces?

Getting Your Money

If you have answered yes to any one of these questions, you may have money waiting for you. This is the best way of insuring that you will have money coming to you.

1) Make a list of every relative you know that has died. If the relative was distant, you may be an heir but only if that relative had few direct descendants.

2) Write the Unclaimed or Treasury Office or phone them. Use the addresses in Chapter 2. Try to provide as much of this information as you can for the state office. Give them your name and address that would be applicable at the time an account in question account was opened. Also include your Social Security number.

3) Your chances are very good if you follow this step. Take the list of all your relatives that have died. Write the Unclaimed or Treasury Office or phone them. Use the addresses in Chapter 2. Try to provide as much of this information as you can for the state office. Give them the (your relative's) account owner's name (maiden name) and address and Social Security number that would be applicable at the time death had occurred. It is wise to include your relationship to the property owner, if that is applicable.

4) When the state office finds money, they will send you claim forms to fill out. After you fill out the forms, the money is yours.

5) The deceased person may have had an insurance policy that you can't locate; to locate it write to:
American Council of Life Insurance 1850 K Street, N.W. Washington, D.C. 2006 Request a free policy search.

6) You or the deceased person may have worked for a city, county or state goverment office. If so you may have earned a pension and not known about it. The next topic will help you get pension money.

Government Employee Retirement Pensions

If you have worked for a city, county or state government office, you may have earned a pension. Working on a part-time basis will not exclude you from earning your pension. If you would like to find out if you or someone else are owed a pension, write or phone the following government offices. Please include the name and address of where you were while employed by them as well as your location and dates of employment, Social Security number, and birth date. Here is the complete list of the offices.

ALABAMA
135 Union Street
Montgomery, Alabama 36130
(205) 832-4140

ALASKA
Department of Administration
Pouch C
Juneau, Alaska 99811
(907) 465-4460

ARIZONA
1777 W. Camelback Road
Phoenix, Arizona 85015
(602) 255-5131

ARKANSAS
One Capitol Mall
Little Rock, Arkansas 72201
(501) 371-1458

CALIFORNIA
1416 9th Street
Sacramento, California 95814
(916) 445-7629

COLORADO
1300 Logan Street
Denver, Colorado 80203
(303) 832-9550

CONNECTICUT
30 Trinity Street
Hartford, Connecticut 06115
(203) 566-2126

DELAWARE
Thomas Collins Building
Dover, Delaware 19901
(302) 736-4208

FLORIDA
Department of Administration
Cedars Executive Center
Building C
Tallahassee, Florida 32303
(904) 488-5541

GEORGIA
Two Northside 75
Atlanta, Georgia 30318
(404) 656-2960

HAWAII
Department of Budget and Finance
888 Mililani Street
Room 502

Honolulu, Hawaii 96813
(808) 548-7593

IDAHO
Office of the Governor
820 Washington Street
Boise, Idaho 83720
(208) 334-3365

ILLINOIS
2815 W. Washington Street
Box 4064
Springfield, Illinois 62708
(217) 753-0444

INDIANA
State Office Building
Room 800
Indianapolis, Indiana 46204
(317) 232-1606

IOWA
Public Employees Retirement
Job Service
1000 E. Grand Avenue
Des Moines, Iowa 50319
(515) 281-5800

KANSAS
400 First National Bank Tower
Topeka, Kansas 66603
(913) 296-3921

KENTUCKY
226 W. Second Street
Frankfort, Kentucky 40601
(502) 564-7986

LOUISANA
Department of the Treasury
PO Box 44213
Baton Rouge, Louisiana 70804
(504) 342-5088

MAINE
State House
Station 46
Augusta, Maine 04333
(207) 289-3461

MARYLAND
Department of Personnel
301 W. Preston Street
Baltimore, Maryland 21201
(301) 383-2344

MASSACHUSETTS
Office of the Treasurer
One Ashburton Place
Boston, Massachusetts 02108
(617) 727-2950

MICHIGAN
Mason Building, 2nd Floor
PO Box 30026
Lansing, Michigan 48909
(517) 373-0001

MINNESOTA
529 Jackson Street
St. Paul, Minnesota 55101
(612) 296-2761

MISSISSIPPI
1704 Sillers Building

Jackson, Mississippi 39202
(601) 354-6191

MISSOURI
PO Box 209
Jefferson City, Missouri 65102
(314) 751-2342

MONTANA
Department of Administration
1712 9th Avenue
Helena, Montana 59620
(406) 449-3154

NEBRASKA
301 Centennial Mall S.
Lincoln, Nebraska 68509
(402) 471-2053

NEVADA
1100 E. William Street
Carson City, Nevada 89710
(702) 885-4200

NEW HAMPSHIRE
6 Loudon Road
Concord, New Hampshire 03301
(603) 271-3351

NEW JERSEY
Department of the Treasury
20 W. Front Street
Trenton, New Jersey 08625
(609) 292-3676

NEW MEXICO
Pera Building

Room 334
Box 2123
Santa Fe, New Mexico 87503
(505) 827-2517

NEW YORK
State Comptroller
A E Smith Buildling
Albany, New York 12244
(518) 474-2600

NORTH CAROLINA
State Treasurer
Albemarle Building
Raleigh, North Carolina 27611
(919) 733-6555

NORTH DAKOTA
316 N Fifth Street
Bismarck, North Dakota 58505
(701) 224-2975

OHIO
277 E Town Street
Columbus, Ohio 43215
(614) 466-2822

OKLAHOMA
Jim Thorpe Building
Room 580
Oklahoma City, Oklahoma 73105
(405) 521-2381

OREGON
1099 S W Columbia
Portland, Oregon 97207
(503) 229-6176

PENNSYLVANIA
Labor and Industry Building
Room 204
Harrisburg, Pennsylvania 17120
(717) 787-6780

RHODE ISLAND
Department of the Treasury
198 Dyer Street
Room 101
Providence, Rhode Island 02903
(401) 277-2203

SOUTH CAROLINA
Blatt Building
Box 11960
Columbia, South Carolina 29211
(803) 758-8952

SOUTH DAKOTA
Department of Labor
Foss Building
Pierre, South Dakota 57501
(605) 773-3731

TENNESSEE
Department of Treasury
Andrew Jackson Building
13th Floor
Nashville, Tennessee 37219
(615) 741-7063

TEXAS
Box 13207
Capitol Station
Austin, Texas 78711
(512) 475-6431

UTAH
540 E Second Street
Salt Lake City, Utah 84111
(801) 355-3884

VERMONT
State Administration Building
Montpelier, Vermont 05602
(802) 828-2305

VIRGINIA
Supp Retirement System
11 N Sixth Street
Richmond, Virginia 23219
(804) 786-3831

WASHINGTON
1025 E Union Street
Olympia, Washington 98504
(206) 753-5290

WEST VIRGINIA
Capitol Complex 5
Room 148
Charleston, West Virginia 25305
(304) 348-2031

WISCONSIN
Employee Trust Funds
201 E Washington Avenue
Room 151
Madison, Wisconsin 53702
(608) 266-3285

WYOMING
Retirement System Board
Barrett Building

Cheyenne, Wyoming 82001
(307) 777-7691

AMERICAN SAMOA
Deparment of Manpower Resources
Utulei
Pago Pago, American Samoa 96799
633-5456 (*No area code)

GUAM
Retirement Fund
Box 3 C
Agana, Guam 97910
(671) 472-6627

M. MARINA ISLANDS
Retirement Building Fund
Box 222, CHRB
Saipan, CM 96950
Overseas 9310

PUERTO RICO
Division of Retired Personnel
Minillas Station
Box 42003
Santurce, Puerto Rico 00940
(809) 724-5550

How To Prevent Your Money From Being Lost

By now, you're probably worried that some time in the future you'll forget about money that's yours or due you. To prevent your assets from being abandoned, lost or escheated, make sure you take the following precautions:

Insurance policies

* Tell your attorney and your family about all insurance policies you have.

* Tell the beneficiaries of your policy that they are beneficiaries.

* Keep a record of your policies and their policy numbers; store them in a safe place.

Safe-Deposit Boxes

* Tell your family, attorney and accountant where your safe-deposit box is.

* Pay the box rental when due.

Bank accounts

* Keep track of accounts opened by you, a friend or a relative for your child. These accounts are usually opened when a child is born, is christened, graduates, etc., and, after time, are easily lost track of.

* Make sure your savings account doesn't sit without activity for more than a year. Deposit some money, withdraw some money just make sure the account is 'active.' If you have a passbook account, have a bank teller enter your accrued interest.

* For all CDs (certificates of deposit), note their maturity date on your calendar so you don't forget to claim them when due.

Stocks, Bonds, Interest, Dividends

* Keep records of all stocks and bonds that you own.

* Mark on your calendar the maturation dates of all your bonds.

* If you can vote on issues facing stockholders, do so; vote your proxy card.

* If you change brokers, check your holdings for errors.

The least you can do is to inform everyone you do financial business with if you move, change your name or job, your bank, if you retire, or have problems receiving your mail. To prevent loss, don't trust the postal service with your irreplaceable personal financial assests.

An Important Message

People have paid me thousands of dollars to get all of the information this book contains. This book was written to help people make enormous amounts of money in a short period of time. Many people asked me if I could offer them additional information to aid them in making $2,000 an hour. I have contacts all over the country that keep me posted in reference to 'unclaimed money' developments on the government and local level. These are contacts and sources of information that took me years to develop. Because of this vital information I had access to, I had to form a link between you and the information. This created a definite need for an association. For this reason the 'Money Finders' association was created.

This association will provide you with all the training you will need to make $2,000 an hour. It will also inform you of everything you need to know as well as assist you in guaranteeing you make $2,000 an hour.

Your association membership will include:

1) **Free phone consultation** with any of our 'Money Finders' trained experts to solve all of your problems.

2) **State unclaimed property** lists and state documents drastically reduced in price from what states charge (some states are not included).

3) **A complete revised selection of legal documents** written up by a team of attorneys that are specific toyour state. These documents can insure that you will not have any legal hurdles.

4) **The 'Money Finders' quarterly news letters** are packed with information about the latest research and techniques in retrieving unclaimed money. The latest state laws as well as existing state laws and regulations are discussed.

5) **Personal training and guidance** make sure you can make $2,000 an hour with this proven system.

6) **Twelve monthly fact-filled issues of "People Finders" magazine.** Each issue contains about 70 pages of unclaimed property and information about searching for people. Free unclaimed property lists are included in every issue as well as tips on how to find missing people.

Everything this membership includes will be worth at least $10,000 dollars to you. You'll want to take advantage of this opportunity because I am only allowing 10,000 members nationwide. I don't want to saturate the market. A membership is only $95. At only $95, memberships to this association won't last long.

Join this association and you will see your financial dreams become a reality. Invest the $95 association fee and you will see a remarkable difference in the thousands more you will make.

Steve Schmidt was able to latch on to one unclaimed account of $142,980 with the help of the association. His share of this treasure for seven hours of work was $47,660.

Andre Isadore, a 14-year-old boy got hold of 30 unclaimed property owner's names. For four hours of simple research and some tips from the association, Andre was able to secure the sum of $16,212.

If you would like to join this association send $95 to:

David Bendah
6602 El Cajon Blvd. Suite 'B'
San Diego, CA 92115

If you are interested please contact me at (619) 265-8777. I would be more than happy to discuss this program with you.

Best wishes,

David Bendah

David Bendah

FIND 'EM FAST: A Private Investigator's Workbook

Rarely is so much truly practical info offered in one book! It's all here — forms, how-to steps for collecting data, and a list of invaluable sources of information. Here are the worksheets and the accompanying text on how to use them — the same information that real private investigators need. And that's not all: there are also methods for getting data on every case, straight from working pro John McCann. Included is a forty-three page 'source of information' section, an indispensable addition to your files. Chapter topics are background and preemployment investigation, civil litigation, surveillance, investigative photography, tips for setting up your own agency, and more. 168 pp. $15

TRACE YOUR FAMILY ROOTS

Genealogy is one of America's fastest-growing hobbies. It also happens to be a major mainstay for private investigators. Millions of dollars are spent nationwide each and every year in the search for ROOTS. This great new book explains in easy-to-understand instructions: how and where to get started; how to keep records; where to write for all kinds of documents and records including birth, death, marriage, deeds, divorce, wills, land transactions, passenger lists, old court transcripts, census schedules, military records, and much more. This is a valuable addition to your skip-tracing library. $10

YOU CAN FIND ANYONE

Legally obtain confidential postal and DMV records; get unlisted telephone numbers; locate birth, death and credit records; find out about county, state and federal court records. Included in this guide are 21 secret information sources and files; find people who don't want to be found. Locate military personnel, active and retired. Search out missing heirs, old friends, lost children, birth parents, debtors, and much, much more. NEWLY REVISED 140 pp. $15

THE PRACTICAL GUIDE FOR PRIVATE INVESTIGATORS

This book presents straight facts on these subjects, plus six Final Examinations to test your working knowledge of the detective business. Other topics include: understanding criminal and civil law; interrogation; surveillance; equipment and training; undercover work; homicide, arson, and divorce investigations; much more. Here you have a source for technical training methods and material, informative lists, and even a look at job opportunities all in one complete guide. 144 pp. $13

#0633

Free Grants & Low-Interest Loans

Lloyd Sanders

Have you ever wondered how people with credit ratings lower than yours obtain money? The only difference between them and you is that they know how and where to get the money. Every year billions of dollars are given to people just like you. Would you like to stake your share? You can, by owning one of the most complete books on money-financing systems. It shows you how to get money from almost every possible source available. Hundreds of methods of raising money are covered in this book.

- Get up to $500,000 in easy-to-qualify SBA loans
- Get up to $350,000 if you're in business and handicapped
- Get up to $315,000 in low-income assistance
- Raise $50,000 with no collateral
- Borrow up to $100,000 from any commercial bank
- Raise up to $50,000,000 the corporate way
- Get up to $67,000 for a home purchase
- Get up to $5,000 a year for education
- Get up to $92,000 for home improvements
- Get up to $150,000 if you are a woman in business
- Learn loopholes in bank policies
- Use creative financing to raise large amounts of capital
- Use advanced banking techniques to get loans
- 270 foundations that will give you a free grant
- Get some of the $3 billion given out by foundations every year
- Get money from 300 financial institutions that loan by mail

These are just some of the money-raising techniques included. *Free Grants & Low-Interest Loans* must contain almost every known method of raising money. Each 5½-by-8½-inch book is $7.

#1855

Get Rich With No Work

David Holmes & Joel Andrews

You can get rich without working by using the multi-level approach. Let me explain it. Your agents get the product from the company, but you get the commission from your agents and each agent they enlist. Others do the work while you sit back and collect the high commissions. Thousands of people just like you are making more than $100,000 a year without working. Once you have this book you can begin to create your fortune with any product you choose.

Holmes and Andrews, the authors, have a combined 20 years of sales and marketing experience. Holmes, a marketing expert and author of two books, has made more than 150 television and radio appearances over the past year. Andrews, who has personally launched six successful business ventures, is so highly regarded in sales and marketing that he has testified on marketing to both Houses of Congress. Together, these men teach you how to get rich without working.

#0333

$200,000 In 24 Hours & 130 Other Moneymaking Reports

Did you ever wonder what companies give you when they offer to make you an instant millionaire overnight? When they offer you instant credit regardless of your past? Well, now for the first time, almost every moneymaking plan and idea on the market has been compiled into one package with reproduction rights, so you can reproduce all or some of these reports. Here are some of the reports you will receive:

- Raise $200,000 in 24 hours without collateral
- Turn bad credit ratings into AAA-1 credit ratings
- Win oil & gas leases in gov't held public drawings
- Profit from a large list of valuable tax loopholes
- Wipe Out all your debts fast without bankruptcy
- Get Rich in mail order, many complete programs
- Stop Paying property taxes! Forever, legally
- Free Subscriptions To More Than 100 Magazines
- Borrow $50,000,000 on your signature for any purpose
- Get Free car, food, clothing, furniture, rent...
- Produce cheap, whiskey, rum, gin, vodka & other liquors
- Convert Your TV into a movie-size screen TV
- Get auto fuel for 15 cents a gallon or produce gasohol
- Purchase a new car for Only $50 above dealer's cost
- Get a $1,000,000 life insurance policy with no cash
- Get an expensive mansion Without Cost
- Get Free Canadian land • Free oil for your car
- Take over a going business with Zero Cash
- Get 300% more on your savings account
- Get gov't land $2.25 an acre • Free Airline Travel
- Strike It Rich with gov't assistance (minerals)
- Own a $1,000,000 corporation in 4 weeks for Only $50
- Buy Gov't Surplus 2 cents on the dollar
- Buy valuable apt., homes & land for next to nothing
- Get All The Credit Cards you will ever want

This is only a small fraction of the reports included. Your kit includes more than 130 full-length reports with reproduction rights.

#1233

Making $500,000 A Year In Mail Order

David Bendah

If you ever dreamed of having your mailbox crammed with thousands of envelopes each containing a check in your name, working any hours you want, whenever you want, and being able to afford the pleasures life has to offer in one of this country's most lucrative businesses, then this book can make those dreams a reality.

Many people, including the author, have made a lot of money in mail order. Mail order is one of the most lucrative businesses you can get involved in. Work in your home, part-time if you want, to realize your life-long dreams of security.

Bendah's book is full of helpful, easy-to-understand information. Bendah, considered one of the nation's leading ad writers, teaches laymen how best to use his unique techniques and explains every aspect of book formation and marketing. He even goes so far as to print his confidential ad results from the many successful mail order ads he has run. He discloses his secret formula that has ensured the success of many mail order businesses. If you ever had a dream of making it big in mail order, *Making $500,000 A Year In Mail Order* can be your key.

#2655

How To Get Rich In Mail Order

Melvin Powers

This book will help you run your business and add to your knowledge of mail order. To do well in this business, you must learn from those who have made a lot of money doing what you want to do, such as Melvin Powers, author of *How To Get Rich In Mail Order*. Extensively experienced, Powers has made millions selling more books by mail than any other publishing company in the world. In fact, he sells 400 different titles by mail. I recommend this book because it specializes in mail order book selling.

Powers' book is well written, full of helpful, easy-to-understand information, and is used extensively to teach college students how to master the art of mail order selling. It has 326 8½-by-11-inch pages, and costs $16.

#2455

Building A Mail Order Business

William Cohen

Another book I recommend highly is *Building A Mail Order Business, A Complete Manual For Success,* by William Cohen. This book is hard bound and 495 pages. It covers every aspect of selling by mail, from the basics to the most sophisticated techniques for increasing sales. Every method is explained in a detailed, logical fashion that shows you, step-by-step, how to do it and do it right. This is one of the most complete up-to-date guides on mail order. Cohen covers product selection, writing, graphics, competition and the legal aspects of mail order. This complete mail order manual is available for only $20.

#2155

999 Little-Known Businesses That Can Make You A Fortune

William Carruthers

This book is a collection of 999 businesses that have made their owners rich. It shows you how hundreds of your ordinary talents can be converted into cash and your own business. The majority of ideas require little or no capital and can be started in your spare time. It gives you such a large variety of projects to undertake that you are sure to find that perfect moneymaker for you. Each plan has been carefully selected as a little-known, unfamiliar business that is completely overlooked in most areas of this country. Each is free of competition and has a personality all its own. Use this book to create that special business that will make you financially independent. This book is 5-by-8-inches and has 258 pages.

#1633

The Self-Publisher's Opportunity Kit

The Self-Publisher's Opportunity Kit contains eight interesting books—they've all been tested and are proven sellers. Each book comes with a copyright agreement, which allows you to reprint and sell as many copies as you wish, and complete, step-by-step instructions on how to market these books for the greatest profit.

In addition to the eight titles, you get proven-effective classified ads and a sales letter to promote your books. Some of the books measure 24, 8½-by-11-inch pages.

The eight books are:

1. How To Get Free Grants
2. Importing—Your Key To Success
3. Making A Fortune With Real Estate
5. The Secret Of Raising Money
6. The Millionaire's Secret Of Growing Rich
7. How To Influence People And Win Them Over
8. How To Get $200,000 In Benefits From The U.S. Gov't

The Self-Publisher's Opportunity Kit, with eight books, certificate of reprint rights, step-by-step instructions, sales letter and classified ads, is only $30.

Make A Fortune & Travel Absolutely Free!

Ben & Nancy Dominitz

#1955

Have you heard about the fat commission checks and free travel benefits in the travel business? This book reveals how you can do both without using a dime of your own money. This book shows you how to:

- Start your travel business out of your home in your spare time
- Add a minimum of 50% to your present income
- Travel free, a guest of air and cruise lines and tour companies
- Receive a discount on all airline tickets and hotel bills
- Make a fortune with group travel and much, much more

Use this book to start a new profitable business or just to save money on all your travels. Get this complete hard-bound, 209-page, 9½-by-6½-inch guide for only $20.

The Self-Publishing Manual

Dan Poynter

#1355

Promoting your self-published book is easy if you have a good guide to follow. One of the best books on self-publishing is *The Self-Publishing Manual*, by Dan Poynter, who has been in the publishing industry for many years. He has published numerous books that have been great successes. Informative and complete, Poynter's 352-page book is a constant reference on the writing, printing, publishing, marketing and distribution of books. If you plan to write and publish soon, you will find this manual invaluable. He covers all aspects of publishing in such detail that his book is considered the bible of the self-publishing industry. This book is a winner at $15.

How To Use Your Hidden Potential To Get Rich

David Bendah

#0433

This book presents a program that clearly maps the route self-made millionaires took to make their fortunes. Any very successful person who has made millions has used the techniques in this book.

Hidden Potential will show any individual, regardless of skill, intelligence and experience, how to use the mind to realize both business and personal dreams.

A complete success program, it is illustrated with charts and diagrams that enable understanding of the mind-transformation process. Included are quizes that monitor the reader's progress to wealth. David Bendah, the author, backs up his points with interesting examples of how ordinary people—from Milton Hershey to William Colgate—used the same techniques to make fortunes. Bendah also devotes three chapters to Japanese wealth-building techniques. In short, this volume is designed to expose the reader to every success principle needed to get rich.

How To Write A Good Advertisement

Victor Schwab

#1455

The more books on advertising you study, the better you will be at writing ads. One book I especially recommend is *How To Write A Good Advertisement, A Short Course In Copywriting,* by Victor O. Schwab, one of the best copywriters of this century. He created many famous ads—one, for *How To Win Friends And Influence People,* sold 5 million copies for author Dale Carnegie.

Schwab's techniques are continuously studied by the top advertising agencies, and you should study them, too. Instead of focusing on the structure of the successful ad, Schwab concentrates on the psychology of the consumer. If you know what consumers want and need, your ads will do very well. After reading this book, you should be able to pinpoint the precise needs of your customers and know how to fulfill them. This 227-page, 8½-by-11-inch detailed book can be yours for only $16.